HIKE

Santa Barbara

by

John McKinney

www.TheTrailmaster.com

Acknowledgments: For long ago introducing me to the joys of hiking the Santa Barbara front country and backcountry, a big thanks to my good friend Bob McDermott. I've appreciated the companionship (and trail updates) from my friends and hikers from the 'hood, Bungalow Haven. I'm grateful to the late Jim Blakely and Bob Easton who generously shared their knowledge of Santa Barbara history and natural history. And thanks to the Santa Barbara school kids (and their parents and teachers) I've led on hikes; nothing is more rewarding than sharing the wonderful local trails with the next generation of hikers.

ISBN-13: 978-0-934161-45-9
Maps designed by Mark Chumley
Cover and interior design by Christian Ophus
Layout and e-book by Lisa DeSpain
Cover photo by Cara Moore
HIKE Series Editor: Cheri Rae
Published by: Olympus Press and The Trailmaster, Inc.
www.TheTrailmaster.com (Visit our site for a complete listing of all Trailmaster publications, products, and services)

Table of Contents

Santa Ynez Mountains

MAP LEGEND

- - - Trail
= = = Dirt road
═ Paved road
▬ Highway
■ Point of Interest
▲ Mountain Peak
∩ Campground

Introduction

HIKE SANTA BARBARA

Some of the very best hiking in Southern California is along trails through the mountain canyons right behind Santa Barbara and Montecito. The creekside paths, the mountain tracks, and the marvelous views of the Pacific, the islands and "America's Riviera," add up to world-class walking.

After college, I moved to Santa Barbara and have lived here and hiked here ever since. I've been blessed to make a career out of being a hiking expert and for the opportunity to walk about and write about trails across the state and around the nation.

No matter how far I roam, it's great to get back to the trails near home. The Santa Ynez Mountains are my home mountains, where I hike with friends and family, where I hike alone to re-focus my thoughts and restore my spirit. I love leading hikes for Santa Barbara school kids, faith-based groups and conservation organizations, as well as for private groups and companies.

I wrote ***HIKE Santa Barbara*** to share my favorite trails with locals and with the city's many visitors from all over Southern California and from all over the world. This MiniBuk is an opinionated guide to hikes you're sure to like, not an exhaustive detailing of every trail.

The wild side of Santa Barbara has long been an attractive destination for visitors and residents alike. At the start of the 20th century, the Hot Springs Hotel in Hot Springs Canyon was an internationally famed destination. And when visitors weren't taking the healing waters they were taking hikes to Cold Spring Canyon, San Ysidro Canyon, Mission Canyon and Inspiration Point.

Even the Santa Barbara Chamber of Commerce has long encouraged hiking in the local mountains. In 1902 it promoted "Chamber of Commerce Trail," though hikers of that era preferred "Rattlesnake Canyon Trail," and that's how the trail through Rattlesnake Canyon is known today.

Just as they impressed earlier generations of hikers, the Santa Ynez Mountains charm the modern hiker with antiquarian oaks and sycamores lining the canyons and a host of seasonal creeks washing the hillsides. In spring, the chaparral blooms and adds frosty whites and blues to the gray-green plants. The mountains look particularly inviting after the first winter rains.

Not all is beautiful on the trails behind Santa Barbara. Hillsides were scorched by the Tea Fire and Gap Fire in 2008 and by the Jesusita Fire in 2009. San Roque Canyon, Rattlesnake Canyon, Mission Canyon and the Santa Barbara Botanic Garden were among the hiking locales blackened by these blazes. The native chaparral regenerates quickly, however, and it's been astonishing, even to locals, how rapidly the flora has recovered.

The trails generally follow creeks to the top of the range. Typically, Santa Barbara's front country trails start in lush canyon bottoms, zigzag up the dry canyon walls, and follow rock ledges to the crest. Many of the trails intersect Camino Cielo (the Sky Road), which follows the mountain crest. From the top, enjoy sweeping views of the Pacific and Channel Islands, the city and coastal plain.

The trails are usually kept in pretty good shape thanks to the volunteer efforts of local hikers and trails groups such as the Montecito Trails Foundation that keeps a watchful eye on some 150 miles of trail. I've described a variety of hikes from easy nature walks to challenging adventures. Many of the hikes have options so that you can make the best use of your time on the trail.

From the viewpoints, hikers can decipher the region's confusing orientation; that is to say, the east-west direction of the coastline and the mountain ranges. Even veteran SoCal hikers can get momentarily baffled when looking south to the ocean. And when the sun seems to set in the north, well, that really confuses visiting hikers! Geographically challenging the range may be, but that soft south light illuminating the mountains makes them all the more magical.

When Santa Barbarans say they are "going over to the valley" what they are going over is the

Santa Ynez Mountains and what they are going over to is the Santa Ynez Valley. Along with Santa Barbarans, legions of visitors from across the nation and around the world are going over to the valley these days.

They go to the valley for two reasons: to sample internationally acclaimed wines and to savor the valley's stunning scenery, a rustic region of ranches and vineyards framed by bold mountain ranges. The Trailmaster suggests a third reason to go to the Santa Ynez Valley: good hiking. The hiking includes trails along the back side of the Santa Ynez Mountains along the Santa Ynez River; a few paths in the wine country itself (though public parkland is scarce) and the high country around Figueroa Mountain, complete with conifers and fabulous vistas.

Hike smart, reconnect with nature and have a wonderful time on Santa Barbara's best trails.

Hike on.

–John McKinney

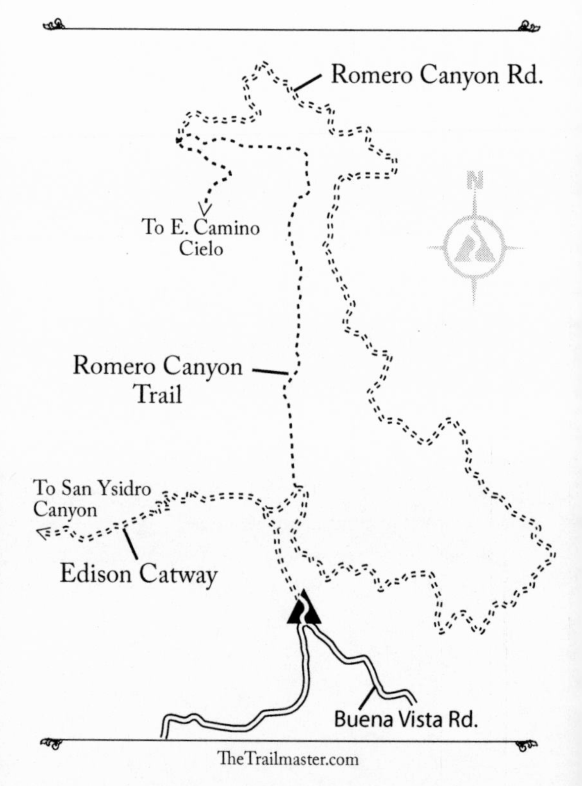
Romero Canyon Rd.
To E. Camino Cielo
N
Romero Canyon Trail
To San Ysidro Canyon
Edison Catway
Buena Vista Rd.

ROMERO CANYON

Romero Canyon Trail

From Bella Vista Road around Romero Canyon is a 6-mile loop with 1,500-foot elevation gain

Romero Canyon is the most easterly of the delightful canyons in the Santa Ynez Mountains back of Santa Barbara. Oaks and sycamores shade a year-round creek and a tranquil path.

Romero Canyon was named for the Romero family, whose first members came to the Santa Barbara area more than two hundred years ago. Juan Romero was a soldier with Governor Felipe de Neve (first resident governor of California) and Captain Jose Francisco Ortega, who helped found El Presidio Real de Santa Barbara in 1782.

One meaning of romero in Spanish is "pilgrim" and pilgrims of several levels of hiking ability will enjoy a walk through Romero Canyon. Families with small children will enjoy sauntering along its lower creekside stretches. More serious hikers will utilize fire roads to make a moderately graded loop through the canyon.

DIRECTIONS: From Highway 101 in Montecito, a few miles down-coast from Santa Barbara, exit on Sheffield Drive. Turn right on Sheffield Drive, which briefly parallels the freeway, then swings sharply left (north) toward the Santa Ynez Mountains. Drive 1.5 miles to East Valley Road. Turn left, proceed 50 yards, then make an almost immediate right on Romero Canyon Road. A half mile along, be sure to veer right at a fork in the road, and continue another mile farther to Bella Vista Road. Turn right and continue 0.25 mile to a red steel gate on the left side of the road. Park in a safe manner alongside Bella Vista Road one of the few spaces in the deeply rutted lot at the trailhead.

THE HIKE: Walk around the gate and head up canyon on the fire road. After 0.25 mile, cross a concrete bridge over Romero Creek. A west-forking trail heads steeply off to San Ysdiro Canyon. You'll cross the creek again, this time without a bridge, and shortly thereafter look for signed Romero Canyon Trail on your left.

The trail follows the right side of Romero Creek, lined with grasses, sedges, sweet-smelling bay laurel and tangles of vines, as well as picturesque old oaks. Crossing over to the left side of the creek and continues a quarter mile or so to another crossing where you'll find a pretty little waterfall spilling into a fern- and moss-lined pool.

Ascending moderately to steeply, the trail crosses the creek a couple more times, then climbs briskly via switchbacks to a signed 4-way trail intersection.

Turn right where the trail intersects the dirt road and begin your long descent. After 2 miles of walking, the road offers views of Montecito estates and the coastline, Anacapa and Santa Cruz Islands. The road intersects Romero Canyon Trail 0.5 mile from the trailhead and you retrace your route on Romero Canyon Road.

San Ysidro
Canyon Trail
N
Falls
Catway
Buena Vista
Connector
Saddle Rock
Girard
Loop
Overlook
Hot Springs
Trail
Old Pueblo
Trail
McMenemy
Trail
Mountain Dr.
Buena Vista Rd.
Park Ln.

San Ysidro Canyon

San Ysidro Trail

From East Mountain Drive to San Ysidro Falls is 3.6 miles round trip with 1,100-foot elevation gain

San Ysidro Trail is attractive and typical of Santa Barbara's foothill trails. The classic canyon walk is a family-friendly trip along San Ysidro Creek to some lovely pools and a small waterfall. Connector trails lead west to Santa Barbara's attractive and best-known canyons—Hot Springs and Cold Spring.

Surrounded by 500 lush acres of its own and many thousands of acres of Los Padres National Forest, San Ysidro Ranch is close to the trailhead and superbly situated for those guests who find hiking, like the ranch, a great way to get away from it all.

A beautiful oak woodland lines San Ysidro Creek. With mighty oaks in the foreground and impressive rock formations in the background, San Ysidro Canyon is a striking scene. Hikers have stacked up rocks to make shallow swimming and wading pools. And then there's pretty, 60-foot San Ysidro Falls, a worthy destination indeed. More serious hikers will sweat up the switchbacks to Camino Cielo, the Sky Road.

DIRECTIONS: From Highway 101 in Montecito, take the San Ysidro Road off-ramp. Drive north on San Ysidro a mile to East Valley Road, turn right and drive a mile to Park Lane, which appears on the left just after crossing San Ysidro Creek. Turn left on Park Lane and in 0.5 mile veer left onto East Mountain Drive. Ignore the first trailhead you see on the right (Winman Trail) and continue 0.2 mile to the end of road (at the boundary with San Ysidro Ranch). Parking for signed San Ysidro Trail is alongside East Valley Road.

THE HIKE: The trail, lined with sea fig, bougainvillea, and other exotic plants, parallels a driveway for a time, passes a couple houses, then becomes a dirt road. Signs direct you back and forth from road to trail. About 0.4 mile out, you'll pass the right-forking Old Pueblo Trail and, in another 0.1 mile, the left-forking McMenemy Trail.

The ascent continues and at 1.4 miles the trail approaches San Ysidro Creek, where in the wet season you'll see a large pool and small waterfall. San Ysidro Trail climbs, a pipe railing lining a steep section of the path. Just over two miles from the trailhead, the trail crosses the creek, where there is often a good-sized pool. One path curves right, but you'll go straight on another path and very soon spot San Ysidro Falls.

Those hikers heading for the upper stretches of San Ysidro Canyon and East Camino Cielo will leave the creek behind and follow the steep rocky trail. Continue marching through the chaparral up long, steep switchbacks. During the ascent, geology buffs will look up at the Matilija sandstone, which has been wind-sculpted into striking cliffs and bluffs. It's a 2.5 mile-trek (with 1,700 feet of elevation gain) to East Camino Cielo.

San Ysidro
Canyon Trail
N
Falls
Catway
Buena Vista
Connector
Saddle Rock
Girard
Loop
Overlook
Hot Springs
Trail
Old Pueblo
Trail
McMenemy
Trail
Mountain Dr.
Buena Vista Rd.
Park Ln.

Buena Vista

San Ysidro, Buena Vista, Old Pueblo Trails

From East Mountain Drive to Buena Vista Overlook is 4.5 miles round trip with 800-foot elevation gain

San Ysidro Ranch has long been known for its romantic, bougainvillea-draped cottages, and an atmosphere that manages to be simultaneously rustic and elegant. Far less-well known are the many captivating hiking trails that begin at a (public) trailhead right next to the upscale hostelry.

Thanks to the efforts of local trails advocates, including the Montecito Trails Foundation, a fine system of pathways leads through and around San Ysidro Canyon.

The classic hike is family-friendly meander to a waterfall (see San Ysidro Canyon hike account);

for something a little different, try some of the pathways leading eastbound out of San Ysidro Canyon. Fashion a loop with the aptly named Buena Vista Trail or head out on an all-day adventure over to Romero Canyon.

DIRECTIONS: From Highway 101 in Montecito, take the San Ysidro Road offramp. Drive north on San Ysidro a mile to East Valley Road, turn right and drive a mile to Park Lane, which appears on the left just after the bridge over San Ysidro Creek. Turn left on Park Lane and in a half-mile veer left onto East Mountain Drive, which passes through a residential neighborhood, then dead-ends at San Ysidro Creek and the back of San Ysidro Ranch.

THE HIKE: Head up San Ysidro Canyon 0.7 mile to Buena Vista Catway Trail (an old road) and turn east. After a few brief moments of mellow hiking, it's gut-check time; the trail suddenly climbs toward the sky. A heart-pounding, 20- to 30-minute ascent leads to a shale-lined saddle.

When your breathing and heart rate returns to normal, take satisfaction that a majority of the climb is behind you. The old roadway gives way to a footpath, which switchbacks down into Buena Vista Canyon.

The trail crosses a little creek to a signed junction. Bear left for the half-mile journey to Buena Vista Overlook. Rest on the stone bench and enjoy coastal and mountain views.

(Beyond the overlook you can continue another 1.5 miles on the ridgeline then descend into Romero Canyon and link up with that canyon's trail system.)

Retrace your steps from the overlook back down into Buena Vista Canyon. Join Buena Vista Trail and descend a mile through a lush, sycamore-shaded canyon and past some striking sandstone boulders.

The simplest way to close the loop is to descend paved Park Lane Road then East Mountain Drive back to the trailhead. True hikers, and those dogged about making loop trails, will leave Park Lane and join Old Pueblo Loop Trail for the mile-long jaunt back to San Ysidro Canyon and the trailhead.

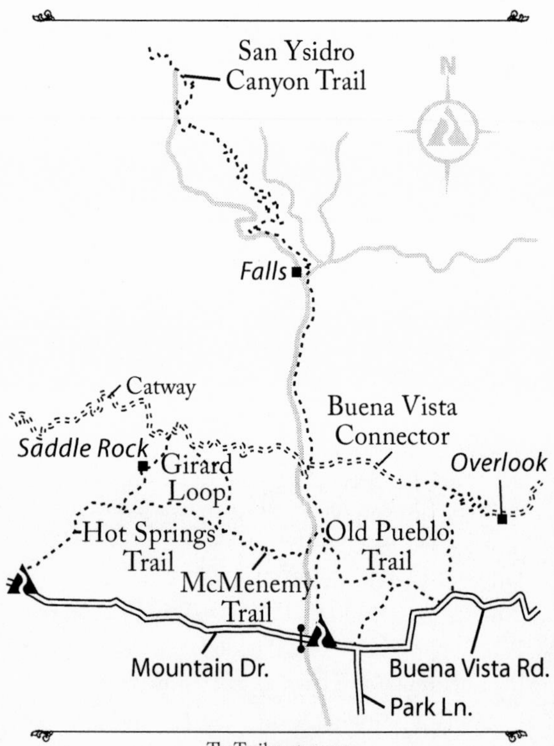
San Ysidro
Canyon Trail
N
Falls
Catway
Buena Vista
Connector
Saddle Rock
Girard
Loop
Overlook
Hot Springs
Trail
Old Pueblo
Trail
McMenemy
Trail
Mountain Dr.
Buena Vista Rd.
Park Ln.

Montecito Connections

San Ysidro, McMenemy, Girard, Saddle Rock Trails

From East Mountain Drive to McMenemy Bench Viewpoint is 2.5 miles round trip with 500 foot elevation gain; Loop via Girard Trail 3.2 miles with 1,000 foot gain; Loop via Hot Springs Canyon is 7 miles round trip

What's not to like about hiking the canyons behind Montecito? Some would say: a lack of connections between canyons.

However, for the hiker in the know, there are good connections and two of Montecito's most attractive canyons—San Ysidro and Hot Springs—can be linked into memorable jaunts.

Canyon connector trails are useful, but not easy to hike. McMenemy Trail, is no walk in the park; Edison Catway climbs steeper than Edison's electricity rates.

DIRECTIONS: From Highway 101 in Montecito, take the San Ysidro Road offramp. Drive north on San Ysidro a mile to East Valley Road, turn right and drive a mile to Park Lane, which appears on the left just after crossing San Ysidro Creek. Turn left on Park Lane and in a 0.5 mile veer left onto East Mountain Drive, which dead-ends near the signed trailhead.

THE HIKE: The trail passes some residences then follows a paved road to a wide dirt one. After about 0.5 mile of travel, you'll pass the signed Old Pueblo Trail ascending east, and then join McMenemy Trail leading west.

The path crosses the creek, leads through a eucalyptus woodland, then embarks on a switchbacking ascent across brushy slopes to the handsome stone McMenemy Bench. Enjoy coastal vistas and ponder your next steps.

My favorite short loop is to join signed Girard Trail, which soon passes steps leading down to an overlook named for trails advocate Edward Girard. It's a steep, 0.5- mile ascent to meet the

Edison Catway. Then it's a short descent east to San Ysidro Trail and a mile back to the trailhead.

For a longer hike, continue west on McMenemy Trail, descending into, and ascending out of, a minor canyon to a ridgetop junction with Saddle Rock Trail.

(Saddle Rock Trail climbs very steeply to a flat-topped vista point where hikers have painstakingly created a heart from small rocks. From "Heart Flat," the path climbs again to Edison Catway, which leads east to San Ysidro Canyon.)

An easier but longer way to go is to continue with McMenemy Trail to Hot Springs Canyon. Just before reaching a dirt road, go around a gate and head up-canyon. The historic road climbs moderately along the east side of Hot Springs Canyon. Just before this byway crosses the creek, swing right and begin a short climb to ruins of the old resort.

Continue onward and upward on Edison Catway to a junction with Saddle Peak Trail and to another junction with Girard Trail, and descend abruptly into San Ysidro Canyon. Cross San Ysidro Creek and enjoy the mellow descent through the canyon back to the trailhead.

East Valley Rd.
East Valley Ln.
Santa Rosa Ln.
N
San Ysidro Creek
San Ysidro Creek Trail
Santa Leandro Ln.

San Ysidro Creek Preserve

San Ysidro Creek Trail

From San Leandro Lane to East Valley Road is 2.5 miles round trip

Montecito, one of coastal California's priciest and most ilyllic residential areas, has a park that seems very much in keeping with its neighborhood. You half expect a gated entry or valet parking for San Ysidro Creek Preserve.

The Land Trust for Santa Barbara County secured 44 acres alongside San Ysidro Creek, a portion of the once sprawling estate of avid polo player Elmer Boeske. After the preserve was established in the late 1980s, some new paths have been constructed and signed by the Montecito Trails Foundation, but otherwise preserve stewards wisely decided to leave well enough alone.

A few miles of pathway explore oak woodland, and meander among rows of olive trees and eucalyptus. This is a preserve set aside for nature study and reflection rather than as a park for picnicking and playing; it's a good place for a quiet walk.

DIRECTIONS: From Highway 101 in Montecito, exit on San Ysidro Road. Head briefly north and make a right on San Leandro Lane. Jog left on Hixon Road, then right again back onto San Leandro Lane, which you follow to a, pumphouse, a white picket fence and San Ysidro Creek Preserve on the north side of the lane. Park carefully along the lane.

THE HIKE: From the white picket fence, wander among the great oaks for 100 yards on the path (aka Ennisbrook Trail) and cross a handsome stone bridge over San Ysidro Creek. After a short half mile, the path emerges from the trees and joins paved Ennisbrook Drive for 100 yards. The trail resumes and drops back to the creek.

After a bit more woodsy walking, you'll cross another stone bridge over San Ysidro Creek and soon reach a junction. Take the left fork, which leads to a cul-de-sac at the end of East Valley Lane. Walk briefly north up the lane to a signed junction with a footpath leading east.

(Those wishing to walk to Montecito's Upper Village, can continue up the lane to it junction with East Valley Road. Turn left (west) and walk 0.5 mile along the road to the village and its shops and restaurants. The road is busier than you'd expect and there's not too much shoulder to walk in places, so be careful.)

Travel among the oaks to another junction. If you proceed straight the path soon crosses San Ysidro Creek, then winds through a eucalyptus forest before it dead-ends a short distance later. The right fork heads south and you'll soon be retracing your steps back to the trailhead.

TheTrailmaster.com

Hot Springs Canyon

Hot Springs Trail

From Hot Springs Road to the Hot Springs Hotel ruins is 3.5 miles round trip with 700-foot elevation gain; return via Cold Spring Canyon is 6 miles round trip with 1,100-foot gain

The attractions for hikers are many: antiquarian oaks and natural beauty of the canyon, the ruins of a hot springs resort, still-active hot springs, and grand vistas of the Santa Barbara coastline and Channel Islands from the high points.

In the early 1880s, a hotel was built in Hot Springs Canyon and attracted spa-goers from around the world. The hotel burned down in 1920, and a smaller private spa burned down in the 1964 Coyote Fire. Since then, bathers have periodically created rock pools and enjoyed the healing waters.

While paths leading through Hot Springs Canyon have been used by hikers for more than a century, the canyon has always been under private ownership and under the threat of development. In 2011, The Land Trust for Santa Barbara County spearheaded a drive to purchase the canyon from the family that owned it for 50 years. The 462-acre property encompasses all of the canyon and local landmark Montecito Peak.

DIRECTIONS: From Highway 101 in Montecito, exit on Olive Mill Road and head toward the mountains. After intersecting Alston Dive, the road continues as Hot Springs Road. Three miles from 101, you'll reach Mountain Drive. Turn left and proceed 0.25 mile to the signed trailhead on the right side of the road.

THE HIKE: The trail climbs moderately through a wooded area, skirting estates and crossing and paralleling private driveways.

After 0.25 mile of travel, you'll leave the villas behind. The trail veers right, dips into the canyon, crosses Hot Springs Creek and joins a dirt road. Pass under ancient oaks and begin the moderate climb along the east side of Hot Springs Canyon.

Notice the stone culverts and the handsome stone retaining walls along the old coach road.

A mile's travel leads to a junction. A left turn puts you on the power-line road that climbs over to Cold Spring Canyon. Stay right, and hike 0.25 mile along the road to the stone steps and other ruins of the Montecito Hot Springs Club. Nearby, exotic flora thrives—bamboo, agave and geraniums, as well as palm, banana and avocado trees—remnants of the landscaped gardens that surrounded the spa during its glory days.

Return the same way, or follow one of two routes to Cold Spring Canyon. Double-back to the above-mentioned road junction and ascend the power-line road to the ridge separating Hot Springs Canyon from Cold Spring Canyon. Or follow the trail above the resort ruins and climb north, then steeply east over the same ridge.

Once atop the ridge, punctuated with power-line towers, descend on unsigned but well-maintained Cold Spring Trail 2 miles through Cold Spring Canyon. The trail ends at Mountain Drive. Turn left and walk a bit over a mile back to your car and the Hot Springs trailhead.

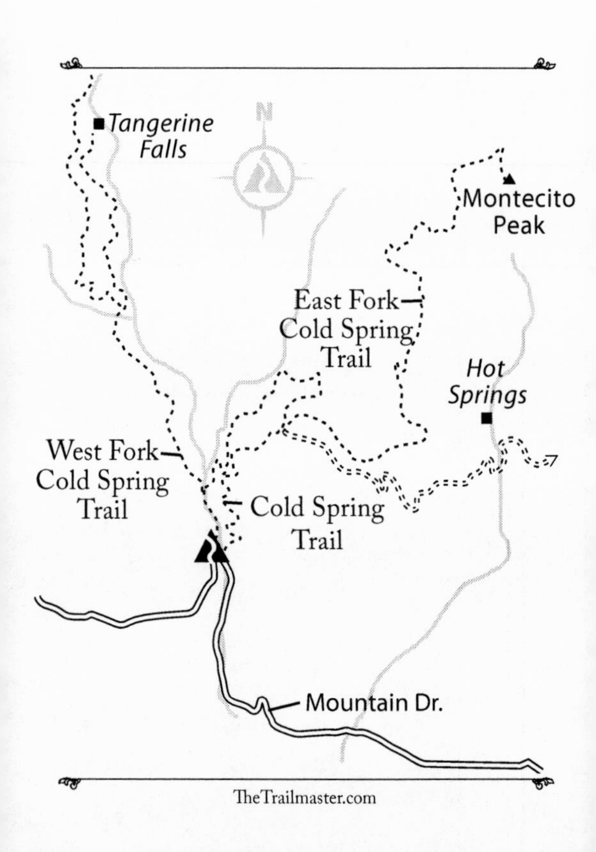

TheTrailmaster.com

COLD SPRING CANYON

Cold Spring Trail

From Mountain Drive to Montecito Overlook is 3.4 miles round trip with 900-foot gain; return via Hot Springs Canyon is a 5.5-mile loop; to Montecito Peak is 7.5 miles round trip with 2,500-foot gain; to Camino Cielo is 9 miles round trip with 2,700-foot gain

Cold Spring Canyon's near-wilderness nature is all the more surprising when considering its location—scarcely a mile as the orange-crowned warbler flies from the villas of the rich and famous, and just two miles from Montecito's boutiques and bistros.

"Our favorite route to the main ridge was by a way called the Cold Spring Trail," wrote Stewart Edward in his 1906 classic, *The Mountains*. "We used to enjoy taking visitors up it, mainly because you come on the top suddenly, without warning. Then we collected remarks. Everybody, even the most stolid, said something."

Cold Spring Trail begins by the alder-shaded, year-round creek, then rises out of the canyon for fine coastal views. Options abound.

DIRECTIONS: From Highway 101 in Montecito, a few miles south of Santa Barbara, exit on Hot Springs Road and proceed toward the foothills for 2.5 miles to Mountain Drive. Turn left. A mile's travel on Mountain Drive brings you to the Cold Springs trailhead, which begins just east of the creek.

THE HIKE: The path rises briefly through oak woodland, then returns to the creek. On your left, 0.25 mile from the trailhead, is a junction with West Fork Trail. (See hike description) East Fork Trail rises up the canyon wall and rejoins the creek 0.5 mile later. Look for a fine swimming hole below you to the right. The trail then switchbacks moderately out of the canyon to Montecito Overlook. Enjoy the view of the Santa Barbara coastline and the Channel Islands.

If you'd like to loop back to the trailhead via Hot Springs Canyon, you have two options.

Easiest way is to take the Edison fire road and make a steep one-mile descent into that canyon. A more challenging route is to ascend Cold Springs Trail another 0.25 mile or so and look for an unsigned connector trail on the right. This path leads down to the ruins of the old Hot Springs Hotel (see Hot Springs Canyon description). Once at the bottom of the canyon, you'll descend a fire road to a vehicle gate, then follow a footpath 0.5 mile around and through a residential area down to Mountain Drive. A mile's walk returns you to the Cold Spring trailhead.

From the junction with the Hot Springs connector trail, Cold Spring Trail switchbacks up-canyon and offers fine coastal views. A one-mile climb brings you to two eucalyptus trees (about the only shade en route!) and another 0.75 mile of travel takes you to the unsigned junction with a side trail leading to Montecito Peak (3,214 feet). Enjoy the view!

Cold Spring Trail continues a last mile to Camino Cielo. From the Sky Road, many trails lead into the far reaches of the Santa Barbara backcountry.

Tangerine Falls
Montecito Peak
East Fork Cold Spring Trail
Hot Springs
West Fork Cold Spring Trail
Cold Spring Trail
Mountain Dr.
N

West Fork, Cold Spring Canyon

West Fork Trail

From Mountain Drive to Tangerine Falls is 3.6 miles round trip with 900-foot elevation gain

Least known and certainly least traveled of Santa Barbara's foothill trails, the West Fork Trail ventures into some surprisingly wild terrain. Bold sandstone formations, clear springs, lush canyon vegetation and a 200-foot waterfall are few of the considerable charms of this branch of Cold Spring Canyon.

A good time to hike the West Fork is after the first heavy rain of winter. The creek's pools bubble over, innumerable newts take to the trail and the canyon's impressive waterfall is a sight to behold.

About that waterfall: it's a natural wonder to view, not visit. Experienced trekkers can follow a sketchy, soggy creekside route to the base of the falls and even beyond, but this is serious, time-consuming business—slow and often very wet going. Don't underestimate the time needed to complete this journey. Many hikers have been stranded up the creek after dark because they got a lot more hike than they bargained for.

DIRECTIONS: From Highway 101 northbound in Montecito, a few miles down-coast from Santa Barbara, exit on Olive Mill Road and drive 2 miles north (toward the mountains) to East Mountain Drive. Turn left and drive a mile to the signed trailhead on the right. Look for the trailhead at a point where Cold Spring Creek flows over a cement drainage apron on Mountain Drive. Parking is along Mountain Drive near the trailhead.

THE HIKE: The trail immediately crosses the creek to the east side of the canyon. It rises briefly through oak woodland, and returns to the creek. Look to your left, 0.25 mile out, for the signed West Fork Trail as well as a small waterfall and a strategically placed bench.

Cross the creek on West Fork Trail and begin a mellow ascent westward under a canopy of oak and bay laurel. Water pipes, historic and modern, parallel the trail.

Just short of a mile from the trailhead, look for an unsigned trail on the right leading down to the creek; this is the rough and sketchy path leading north up the canyon to the waterfall.

Cross a seasonal creek and trek up what is the middle fork of Cold Spring Canyon. The path crosses and re-crosses the creek, past cascades and pools. It's slow going to maneuver (carefully, please) around abandoned water pipes and boulders big and small to get to the base of Tangerine Falls. Enjoy—but don't go climbing up the slippery rocks.

If you want to fully explore the West Fork, return to the main trail. Hike a mile on the trail, which delivers a view of the waterfall then turns away from it as the canyon narrows and the going gets steeper. West Fork Trail ends at a hairpin turn of Gibraltar Road, one of the key access roads into the front country of Los Padres National Forest.

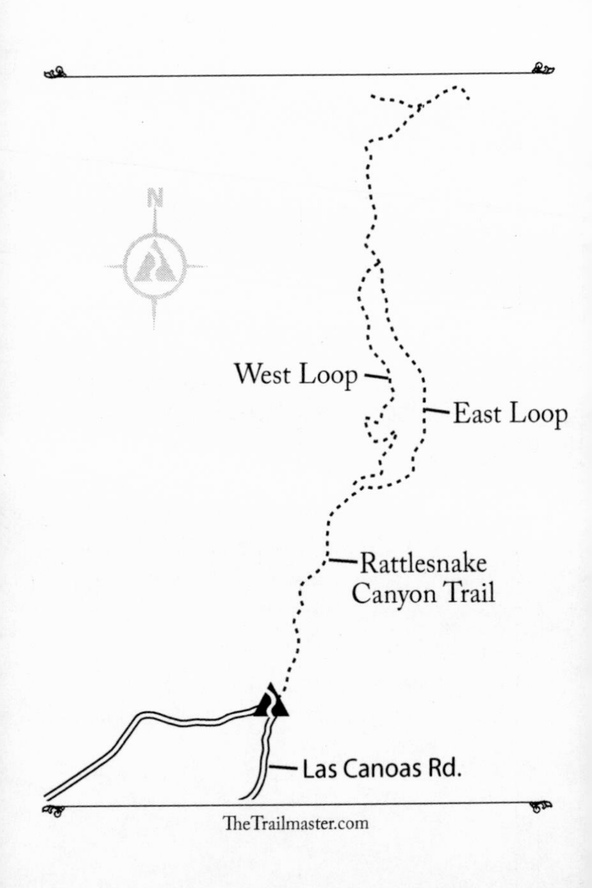
N
West Loop
East Loop
Rattlesnake
Canyon Trail
Las Canoas Rd.

Rattlesnake Canyon

Rattlesnake Canyon Trail

From Skofield Park to Tin Can Meadow is 3.6 miles round trip with 1,000-foot elevation gain; to Gibraltar Road is 6 miles round trip with 1,500-foot gain

Rattlesnake Canyon Trail is serpentine, but otherwise far more inviting than its name.

The joys of hiking the canyon were first promoted by none other than the Santa Barbara Chamber of Commerce. In 1902 the chamber built "Chamber of Commerce Trail," an immediate success with both tourists and locals, though both trail and canyon continued to be called Rattlesnake.

In the 1960s, the city of Santa Barbara purchased the canyon as parkland. A handsome wooden sign at the foot of the canyon proudly proclaims: Rattlesnake Canyon Wilderness.

The canyon was severely burned in the Tea Fire of November 2008, but the chaparral community in particular has recovered quite well from the devastation. Red-berried toyon, manzanita with its white urn-shaped flowers, and purple hummingbird sage cloak the slopes.

DIRECTIONS: In Santa Barbara, follow State Street to Los Olivos Street. Head east and proceed a half mile, passing by the Santa Barbara Mission and joining Mission Canyon Road. Follow this road past its intersection with Foothill Road and make a right on Las Canoas Road, continuing to the trailhead, located near the handsome stone bridge that crosses Rattlesnake Creek. Park alongside Las Canoas Road.

THE HIKE: From the Rattlesnake Canyon Wilderness sign, head north and soon rock-hop across the creek. A brief ascent leads to a trail that parallels the east side of the creek.

After a half mile, an unsigned trail veers off to the right. (One of The Trailmaster's favorite byways, this narrow path leads along and above the east bank of Rattlesnake Creek and reunites with the main trail in about a mile.)

Soon after the junction, the main trail draws near the creek and crosses it. The path then ascends past remnants of a small stand of planted pines and into the open for good vistas of coast and ocean. Continue to a creek crossing and notice (you can't miss it, really) a large flat rock in the middle of the creek known by locals as "Lunch Rock."

The trail crosses the creek again, continuing along the west bank to open, grassy Tin Can Meadow, named for a homesteader's cabin constructed of chaparral framing and kerosene can shingles and sidings. For the first quarter of the 20th century, Tin Can Shack was a canyon landmark, mentioned in guidebooks of that era. A 1925 brushfire destroyed the shack.

The apex of the triangular-shaped meadow is a junction. The trail bearing left leads 0.75 mile and climbs 500 feet to an intersection with Tunnel Trail. To the right, Rattlesnake Canyon Trail climbs 0.75 mile and 500 feet to meet Gibraltar Road. The hiker's reward is an unobstructed view of the South Coast.

Seven Falls
Inspiration Point
Tunnel Trail
Jesusita Trail
N
Tunnel Rd.
S B Botanic Garden
San Roque Rd.
Foothill Rd.
Mission Canyon Rd.

Mission Canyon

Tunnel Trail, Jesusita Trail

From Tunnel Road to Seven Falls is 2 miles round trip with 400-foot elevation gain; to Inspiration Point is 4 miles round trip with 800-foot gain

Seven Falls has long been a popular destination for hikers. "A pleasant party spent yesterday up Mission Canyon visiting noted Seven Falls and afterward eating a tempting picnic dinner in a romantic spot on the creek's bank," the Santa Barbara Daily Press reported in 1887.

This easy family hike follows Tunnel Trail, joins Jesusita Trail for an exploration of the seven little falls and numerous cascades found in the bed of Mission Creek, and ascends to Inspiration Point for sweeping coastal views.

Tunnel Trail was used by workers to gain access to a difficult city waterworks project. Upper Mission Canyon was severely scorched by the

2009 Jesusita Fire. The riparian flora on the canyon bottom looks pretty good; the open slopes along the paved road are recovering more slowly.

DIRECTIONS: From Highway 101 in Santa Barbara, exit on Mission Street. Turn east to Laguna Street, then left and drive past the historic Santa Barbara Mission. From the mission, drive up Mission Canyon Road, turning right for a block on Foothill Road, then immediately turning left back onto Mission Canyon Road. Drive 0.3 mile to a distinct V-intersection, veer left onto Tunnel Road and drive a mile to its end. Park alongside the road. This is a particularly popular trail in the late afternoons and weekends; you might have to park quite some distance down the road from the trailhead.

THE HIKE: From the end of Tunnel Road, hike past a locked gate onto a paved road. Enjoy far-reaching city and ocean views. About 0.75 mile from the trailhead, the road makes a sharp left and crosses a bridge over the west fork of Mission Creek, where a waterfall spills over some boulders.

Beyond the bridge, hike a short distance under handsome oaks to a junction. (Tunnel

Trail angles northeast, uphill, leading three miles to East Camino Cielo.) Join dirt Jesusita Trail, which soon descends to Mission Creek.

At the canyon bottom, you can hike up-creek into a steep gorge that was cut from solid sandstone. Rainwater rushing from the shoulder of La Cumbre Peak has cut away at the canyon's sandstone layers, forming several deep pools. Use caution; reaching the waterfalls—particularly the higher ones—requires quite a bit of boulder hopping and rock climbing. Even when there's not much water in the creek, it can be tricky going. (More cascades and pools are located down-canyon from the trail crossing.)

From the creek crossing, Jesusita Trail switchbacks steeply for one mile up the chaparral-cloaked canyon wall to a T-junction with a power line road atop a knoll. Cross the road, walk a few moments east, and join the path for the 0.2-mile hike down from the ridgeline to Inspiration Point. The view from the cluster of sandstone rocks at the 1,750-foot viewpoint includes a long length of coastline, the Channel Islands, Santa Barbara and the Goleta Valley.

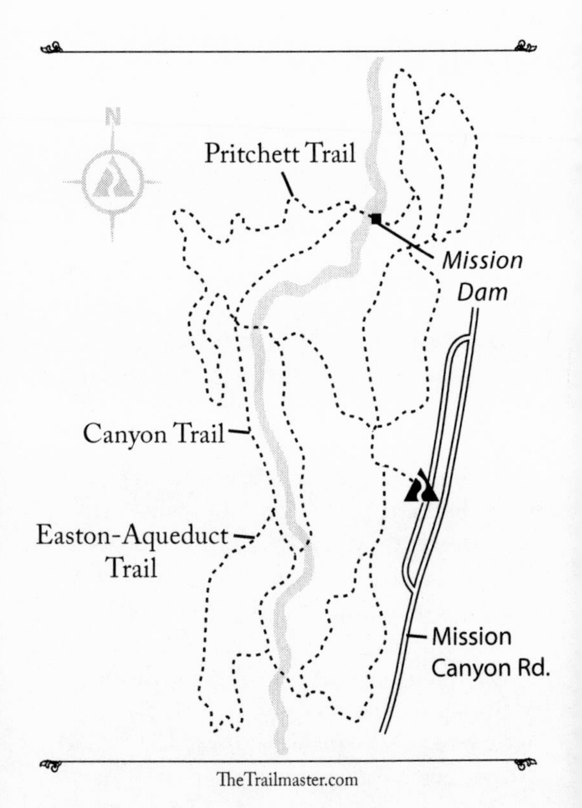
N
Pritchett Trail
Mission Dam
Canyon Trail
Easton-Aqueduct Trail
Mission Canyon Rd.

SANTA BARBARA BOTANIC GARDEN

Canyon, Pritchett, Easton Trails

1 to 3 miles round trip

Nestled in the rugged landscape of Mission Canyon, the Santa Barbara Botanic Garden is truly a treasure, a living museum. Pathways leading through California's ecosystems allow quick getaways from city life. The garden, home to more than 1,000 species of native trees, shrubs and flowers, is a place to linger and learn.

Founded in 1926, this 65-acre enclave is devoted to the display, protection and research of native species. Ecosystems represented include meadows, desert, chaparral, woodland, arroyo, and the Channel Islands. Magnificent redwoods thrive in a grove located on the flat streambed along Mission Creek.

Among the ongoing programs offered by the garden are lectures, docent-led tours, field trips to other gardens, classes and workshops. A herbarium, library, year-round nursery and well-stocked garden bookstore are also attractions to plant lovers.

Easton Aqueduct Trail honors the late Robert Easton, a fourth-generation Californian, fine writer of California-themed books, and long-time conservationist, who worked diligently to protect the South-Central Coast and the Santa Barbara backcountry. I've linked this pathway and several other trails into a clockwise route around the garden. Begin the hike at the main entrance at 1212 Mission Canyon Road. Have fun and improvise: You can make a tight circle for a one-mile walk or take every side trail and enjoy a three-mile excursion.

DIRECTIONS: From Highway 101 in Santa Barbara, exit on Mission Street and head east to Laguna Street. Turn left and, keeping the Santa Barbara Mission on your left, you'll soon join Mission Canyon Road. When you reach a stop sign at Foothill Road, turn right, and then make an almost immediate left back onto Mission Canyon Road. Travel 0.2 mile to a distinct V-shaped intersection. To reach the main entrance:

At the above-mentioned V-intersection, keep right on Mission Canyon Road and follow it a half mile to nearly to road's end, where you'll find the Santa Barbara Botanic Garden. Park in the garden's lot. There is a fee to enter the garden.

THE HIKE: From the garden's main entrance, as you pass the entry kiosk and approach the bookstore, turn left on the brick pathway and walk past the Discovery Garden and the Home Demonstration Garden. Join the path heading down into the canyon. Carefully cross the creek then veer left on signed Easton Aqueduct Trail.

The trail zigzags through the Island Section (plants from the Channel Islands), nears Tunnel Road, then drops to a small bench. Continue on a short descent to Mission Dam and a footbridge over Mission Creek. Enjoy the lovely scene and the restful sound of cascading water.

Join the wide path along the canyon bottom to the redwoods, and then ascend a brick path to the meadow section of the garden. Walk the fringe of the meadow, passing a picnic area, a display of California native orchids, an information kiosk and even a display of desert flora, before returning to the garden shop and entry.

Seven Falls
Inspiration Point
Tunnel Trail
Jesusita Trail
N
Tunnel Rd.
S B Botanic Garden
San Roque Rd.
Foothill Rd.
Mission Canyon Rd.

SAN ROQUE CANYON

Jesusita Trail

To Moreno Ranch is 2.6 miles round trip with 700-foot elevation gain; to Inspiration Point is 6 miles round trip with 1,200-foot gain

Fortunately for hikers, the Depression of the 1930s forced San Roque Country Club to cancel its plans and much of San Roque Canyon became parkland rather than a golf course.

Jesusita Trail extends 4.5 miles east-west from San Roque to Mission canyons. Between the canyons is a high ridge with viewpoints, including official Inspiration Point. Creekside flora, handsome rock formations, avocado orchards, grassy meadows, power lines and panoramic views are all part of the Jesusita experience.

The trail was a flashpoint for the 2009 Jesusita Fire, which burned more than 8,000 acres and destroyed 80 homes. San Roque Canyon's native flora has since recovered somewhat and local volunteers have done wonders to re-hab Jesusita Trail.

DIRECTIONS: From Highway 101 in Santa Barbara, exit on Las Positas Road and drive north two miles. Continue on San Roque Road, 0.4 mile past its intersection with Foothill Road to the Cater Water Filtration Plant.

THE HIKE: Descend Jesusita Trail, soon pasing a left-branching path that leads to Stevens Park. About a half-mile out, hike past a picnic table and at 0.75 mile reach a signed junction. Arroyo Burro Trail forks left; stay right with Jesusita Trail.

The path curves and ascends to an open meadow; follow the narrower path alongs its left edge. About a mile out, cross San Roque Creek, then re-cross it again a few more times. Jesusita Trail parallels a private ranch road and eventually meets it.

Follow trail signs and continue across Moreno Ranch to the top of a hill and a vehicle gate. Pass through a smaller pedestrian gate to a shady vista point, picnic table and a drinking fountain (the only one found along a Santa Barbara Trail!).

Inspiration Point-bound hikers will continue down the dirt road into the shady confines of the canyon. Emerge on open, chaparral-cloaked slopes and get grand views of Santa Barbara and the ocean. Passing handsome sandstone formations, travel under power lines to the ridgeline and a junction with the Edison power-line road.

Head left along the road to meet footpaths leading left (north) and south (right). The leftward path is Jesusita Trail and it leads down intoMission Canyon. Reach Inspiration Point by descending east on the power-line road a short distance.

Look sharply right for a narrow, unsigned connector trail leading 0.2 mile or so to Inspiration Point, a cluster of sandstone boulders. views from the 1,750-foot point include the city and coastlines of Santa Barbara and Ventura.

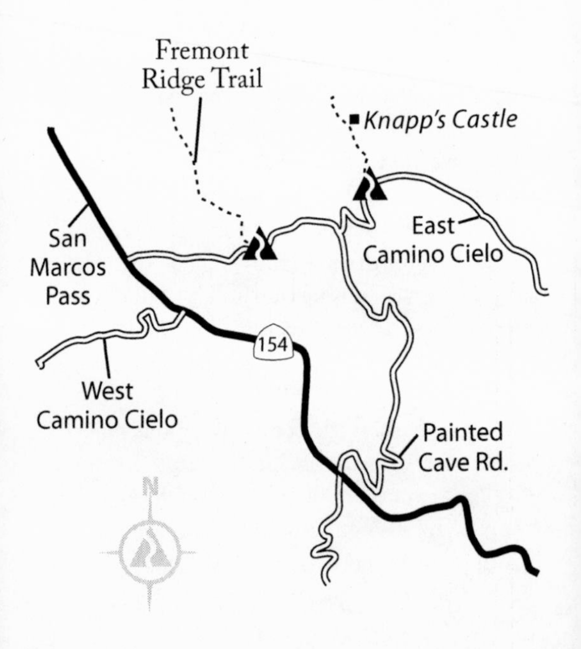
Fremont
Ridge Trail
Knapp's Castle
San
Marcos
Pass
East
Camino Cielo
154
West
Camino Cielo
Painted
Cave Rd.
N

FREMONT RIDGE

Fremont Ridge Trail

From East Camino Cielo to Vista Point is 2 miles round trip with 300-foot elevation gain

Follow in the footsteps of famous pathfinder John C. Fremont to an overlook of the Santa Ynez Valley. In 1846, Fremont led an American Army battalion over the mountains to "save" Santa Barbara from the Spanish Californios.

DIRECTIONS: From Highway 154 near the crest of San Marcos Pass, turn east on East Camino Cielo and proceed 1.75 miles to a metal Forest Service gate on the left and parking.

THE HIKE: After the first 0.25 mile, the steep ridge route is fairly steep mellows. A short mile out, Fremont Ridge begins a drastic decline toward the valley. Savor panoramas of Cachuma Lake and Los Padres peaks and return the way you came.

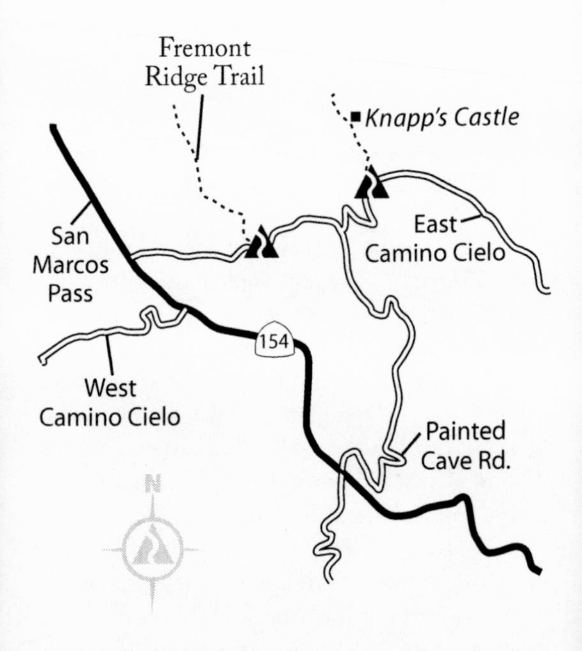
Fremont
Ridge Trail
Knapp's Castle
San
Marcos
Pass
East
Camino Cielo
154
West
Camino Cielo
Painted
Cave Rd.
N

Knapp's Castle

From East Camino Cielo to Knapp's Castle is 1.5 miles round trip with 200-foot elevation gain

In 1916, George Owen Knapp's recurrent bouts of hay fever sent him high into the Santa Ynez Mountains behind Santa Barbara to seek relief. The wealthy, former Chairman of the Board of Union Carbide found relief—and an ideal locale to build the mountain home of his dreams.

"This tract, at the edge of the grand canyon of the Santa Ynez Mountains, is one of the most magnificent, in point of scenic glories, in California," reported the Santa Barbara Morning Press.

Knapp's dream home, carved from thick sandstone blocks, took four years to complete. It was a magnificent residence, complete with illuminated waterfalls and a room housing one of Knapp's other passions—a huge pipe organ.

While Knapp was developing his private retreat, he was also helping to boost public access to the Santa Barbara Forest Reserve, as it was known in those days. Knapp and a couple of his wealthy friends were tireless promoters of roads and trails, in order to make the backcountry accessible to all. As a 1917 editorial in the Santa Barbara Daily News put it: "Under their leadership places in the wild heretofore denied humans because of their utter inaccessibility are being opened up to the hiker and horseback writer."

Knapp was 60-something when he threw himself into his castle-building and trail-building efforts. He spent most of the rest of his long productive life in his castle in the sky. In 1940, he sold his retreat. A forest fire destroyed the castle just five months after he sold it.

Stone walls, part of the foundation and a couple of chimneys are all that remain of Knapp's Castle. But the view of the Santa Barbara backcountry is still magnificent, particularly if you arrive at sunset and watch the purple shadows skim over the Santa Ynez and San Rafael Mountains.

The upper part of the trail, formerly Knapp's long driveway to his retreat, offers an easy walk down to the ruins from Camino Cielo. The current owner has made efforts to stabilize some of the structures and kindly still allows public access.

DIRECTIONS: From Highway 101 in Santa Barbara, exit on Highway 154 and proceed 8 miles to East Camino Cielo. Turn right and drive 2.5 miles to a saddle, where you'll spot a parking area and a locked Forest Service gate.

THE HIKE: Chamise, ceanothus, toyon and other members of the hardy chaparral family line the old road to the castle. Enjoy fine vistas of the Santa Ynez Valley. After 0.5 mile, the castle comes into view and you continue your descent to the unusual and very photogenic assemblage of walls, arches and chimneys.

From the ruins of Knapp's Castle, enjoy the view of the Santa Ynez River, Cachuma Lake and the wide blue Pacific. And take in the panorama of peaks from Mt. Pinos to Figueroa Mountain to the Casmalia Hills.

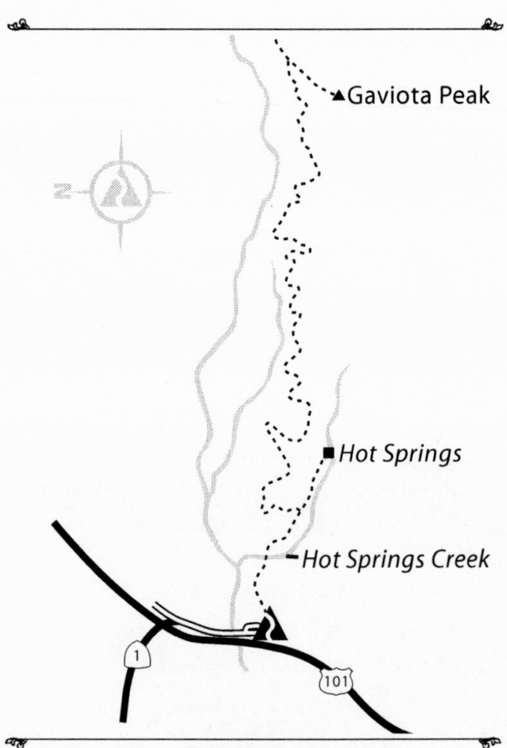
Gaviota Peak
N
Hot Springs
Hot Springs Creek
1
101

GAVIOTA PEAK

Gaviota Peak Trail

From Highway 101 to Gaviota Hot Springs is 1 mile round trip; to Gaviota Peak is 6.2 miles round trip with 2,000-foot elevation gain

Gaviota Peak Trail seems far removed from the other Santa Ynez Mountains footpaths that are so easy to access from downtown Santa Barbara. Located just a half-hour drive from the city, the trailhead and trail seem much farther out of town. Enjoy hiking in the wild west side of the mountains, a contrast to the city's lovely, but sometimes too-popular canyon trails.

The trail leads to warm mineral pools and continues to the top of Gaviota Peak (2,458 feet) for superb coastal views. A wide path curves relentlessly upwards with ever-better vistas of Gaviota Grade, one of the steepest along U.S. 101 in California, and historic Gaviota Pass.

Experienced hikers can fashion two longer loop routes of about 11 miles: Trespass Trail is faint, poorly maintained and weed-choked, but the experienced hiker can stick with it. Campbell Trail has been officially abandoned by the U.S. Forest Service with the explanation that Chumash archaeological sites are in the vicinity. It's not a bad trail per se, but desperately overgrown in places with brush and thickets of poison oak. Corrie Meadow is watered by a tiny creek and splashed with wildflowers in the spring.

DIRECTIONS: Thirty-five miles up coast from Santa Barbara, exit Highway 101 at Lompoc/Highway 1 off-ramp. Turn east a short distance, then follow the highway frontage road 0.25 mile to road's end at the Gaviota State Park lot (fee).

THE HIKE: Follow the fire road, often strewn with rocks and eroded from winter floods. This is a well-used stretch of trail; most folks walk only to the hot springs and turn back. Leaving behind the highway noise, a half-mile walk beneath spreading oaks and old sycamores brings you to a creek crossing and then to a junction.

About a half-mile from the trailhead, when you'll pass a junction with Tresspass Trail and further along, spot the trail leading to the hot springs. (Walk a few hundred yards to a series of lukewarm pools. The blue-gray hued waters have a moderate sulfur content and odor.)

The wide road ascends a grassy hillside for impressive views of Gaviota Pass. Spring wildflower displays on these open slopes can be impressive.

The fire road leaves behind the oaks and enters a chaparral community. Switchbacking along, the road crosses from the state park into the national forest about 1.5 miles from the trailhead and reaches a saddle at the two-mile mark.

Just past an old gate, at the top of the ridge, the road junctions. Leftward, a rough route follows the ridge to the west. Straight ahead, a narrow path drops into San Onofre Canyon. Bear right and ascend 0.1 mile on a narrow trail to Gaviota Peak. On clear days much of the Santa Barbara County coastline, as well as the Channel Islands and Point Conception are visible from the peak.

1
101
Gaviota Peak
Fire Rd.
Yucca Trail
Hollister
Trail
Las Cruces Trail
Trespass
Trail
Woodland
Trail
Overlook
Fire Rd.
Tunnel View
Trail
Gaviota
Pass
N
Beach to
Backcountry
Trail
101

GAVIOTA PASS, GAVIOTA STATE PARK

Beach-to-Backcountry, Overlook, Hollister Trails

To Gaviota Pass Overlook is 5 miles round trip with 700-foot elevation gain; loop via Overlook and Hollister Trails is 8.5 miles round trip with 800-foot elevation gain

Most of the Gaviota Pass—the green scene on either side of Highway 101—is the rolling backcountry of 2,775-acre Gaviota State Park. Park trails meander across oak-dotted potreros and travel ridgetops that afford hikers grand vistas of Gaviota Pass and the wide blue Pacific.

On the west side of the pass, the park's trail network honeycombs a delightful backcountry and offers the hiker a number of loops of varying distances and difficulties.

DIRECTIONS: From Santa Barbara, drive up-coast (west) some 30 miles on Highway 101. Just as the highway makes a dramatic bend north, you'll spot a sign for Gaviota State Park. Carefully turn left across the highway onto the state park entry road. Veer right before the park entry kiosk. At the first bend in the road, find the trailhead and parking.

THE HIKE: Begin on the asphalt road (closed to vehicles), which leads 0.6 mile across thickets of sweet-smelling sage and fennel on a route parallel to Highway 101. Join the left-forking, signed ("Multi-Use Trail") path as it winds its way to the top of a mustard-splashed hillock.

Next the path climbs more earnestly along a rocky ridge. Intriguing sandstone outcroppings protrude above the chaparral. The trail deposits you at the mouth of a large wind-sculpted cave.

Beyond the cave, Beach-to-Backcountry Trail dips and rises another 0.5 mile or so before making a final dip to an unsigned junction with Overlook Fire Road. A right on the fire road leads 0.5 mile to a viewpoint occupied only by an antenna and a small concrete block building.

A three-minute walk left on the fire road leads among grand old oaks to an unsigned junction. The fire road bends right (north) while Hollister Trail heads west. I prefer joining Hollister Trail, which ascends west, then bends north.

The path travels a ridgetop and offers great views over Hollister Ranch and the coastline. After about 0.75 mile, the trail passes a junction with a right-forking connector trail that descends to Overlook Fire Road.

Nearly two miles from its junction with Overlook Fire Road, Hollister Trail reaches a four-way junction. Hollister Trail ascends another 0.25 mile north to a viewpoint, then bends west to the park boundary line.

A right-forking fire road (Las Cruces Trail) descends steeply to a path near, and parallel to, 101; Yucca Trail also descends to this path.

Make a loop trip out of this jaunt by descending on either the trail or the fire road to the footpath near Highway 101. Join an unsigned southbound trail for 0.5 mile to meet Overlook Fire Road and ascend another 0.5 mile to a junction with Beach-to-Backcountry Trail.

To Upper Oso
To Little Pine Mountain
Aliso Loop Trail
Aliso Interpretive Trail
Santa Ynez River
Aliso Creek
Sage Hill Campground
Paradise Rd.
N

Aliso Canyon

Aliso Canyon Nature Trail

3.5-mile loop with 500-foot elevation gain

In a relatively short distance, Aliso Canyon Nature Trail explores a variety of typical back-country plant communities—oak woodland, grassland and chaparral. The canyon takes its name from white and gray-barked sycamores (alisos) that grow in the canyon.

The loop trail follows Aliso Creek and climbs to a ridgetop viewpoint. Because of its importance, the nature trail earned the federal "National Recreation Trail" designation.

Even during drought periods, when the Santa Ynez River is bone-dry, Aliso Canyon is usually green. The spring wildflower display can include purple lupine, golden California poppies and red Indian paintbrush.

DIRECTIONS: From Highway 101 in Santa Barbara, take the Lake Cachuma/Highway 154 exit. About 10 miles from Santa Barbara, just over San Marcos Pass, turn right on Paradise Road and drive 4 miles to the signed turnoff on your left for Los Prietos Ranger Station and Sage Hill Campground on the left. Follow the signs and road to Sage Hill Campground and park in upper end of the camp.

THE HIKE: The trail heads north along the bottom of Aliso Canyon, which is filled with coast live oak and sycamore. You'll cross the creek a couple times and in 0.25 mile pass the signed junction with upper branch of the loop trail, which comes in from the right; this will be your return route.

The trail crisscrosses the creek a number of times. After a mile, the path leaves Aliso Canyon, zigzags east up a steep shale slope, then skirts a lovely meadow. Blue-eyed grass, popcorn flower and California poppies dot the meadow.

At the1.5-mile mark, you'll find a signed junction. (One trail heads straight ahead (east) to Upper Oso Camp and a junction with Santa

Cruz Trail. This trail presents a great opportunity to extend your hike. A mile and a half of travel along Santa Cruz Trail brings you to Nineteen Oaks Camp and four miles of trekking to Little Pine Mountain.)

Take Aliso Canyon Trail right (south) at the junction and switchback up the hill to the high point of the nature trail. Enjoy good views of the Santa Ynez Mountains to the south, the San Rafael Mountains to the north.

The trail descends sage-covered slope to the lip of Santa Ynez Canyon, sculpted long ago by the erosive action of the Santa Ynez River. You get a good view of the river, which can be quite a torrent in wet years. On a summer's day during dry years, the river doesn't look like much—just a few shallow pools—but it's actually the longest stretch of free-flowing river in Southern California.

The trail travels along a precipice for a short time, then switchbacks down to the bottom of Aliso Canyon. Near the canyon mouth, you'll intersect the path where you started, head left, and soon return to the trailhead.

Alexander Peak
Little Pine Mtn.
Santa Cruz Trail
Oso Creek
Nineteen Oaks
Canyon Trail
Aliso Creek
Buckhorn-Camuesa Rd.
Aliso Loop Trail
Upper Oso
Santa Ynez River
River Road

NINETEEN OAKS AND LITTLE PINE MOUNTAIN

Canyon, Santa Cruz Trails

From Upper Oso Camp to Nineteen Oaks Camp is 4 miles round trip with 500-foot elevation gain; to Little Pine Saddle is 10.4 miles round trip with 2,800-foot gain; to Little Pine Mountain is 11.4 miles with 3,300-foot gain

Santa Cruz Trail presents a lengthy climb, but rewards the hiker with superb views of the Channel Islands and the Pacific. The trail tops Little Pine Mountain (4,459 feet).

The first, easy part leads to the quiet pools of Oso Creek and to picnicking at Nineteen Oaks Camp. Upper reaches of the path ascend the hot, exposed slope of Little Pine Mountain. Start trekking in the cool morning when the trail is shadowed and enjoy lunch at the summit.

DIRECTIONS: From Santa Barbara, follow Highway 154 northwest 11 miles over San Marcos Pass. Turn right onto Paradise Road and follow it east for 6 miles along the Santa Ynez River to Lower Oso Campground. Turn left onto Romero Camuesa Road and follow it a mile to Upper Oso Campground and the trailhead at its east end.

THE HIKE: Join Canyon Trail, pass a gate, and ascend into the canyon. High canyon walls tower above the Oso Creek, which you'll cross and re-cross several times as you trek a length of canyon locals call Oso Narrows. A mile out, Canyon Trail meets Santa Cruz Trail; continue up-canyon on this trail.

For the next 0.8 mile, the trail is relatively flat, although it drops in and out of washes on the east side of Oso Creek. Look for a signed spur trail on the right leading 0.2-mile to Nineteen Oaks Camp.

(For a different return route from Nineteen Oaks Camp: double-back a mile, then follow Buckhorn Camuesa Fire Road for another mile back to the trailhead. Bear left at a junction and when the road takes a sharp hairpin turn, continue straight ahead. The road stays just east of Oso Creek and several fine swimming pools.)

Santa Cruz Trail heads north, crosses Oso Creek, and switchbacks through grassy meadows. Dip in and out of brush-smothered canyons, cross patches of gray-green soil (serpentine rock) and ascend a hill to a saddle between the ridge you're traveling and Little Pine Mountain.

The trail switchbacks north, then west across the south face of Little Pine Mountain. Cross two meadows ("Mellow Meadows") and ascend around the heads of half a dozen canyons to reach Little Pine Saddle and a junction.

(Warning: beyond the saddle, Santa Cruz Trail and connector trails are often sketchy, including the connector trail leading to waterless and wildfire damaged Happy Hollow Camp and the overgrown side trail to Little Pine Spring.)

To reach the top of Little Pine, take the trail to the right and hike steeply toward the summit. Bear right again at a wood and wire fence and press onward and upward toward the peak. Great vistas from the dramatic ridgeline: Channel Islands, Santa Ynez Valley, Lake Cachuma.

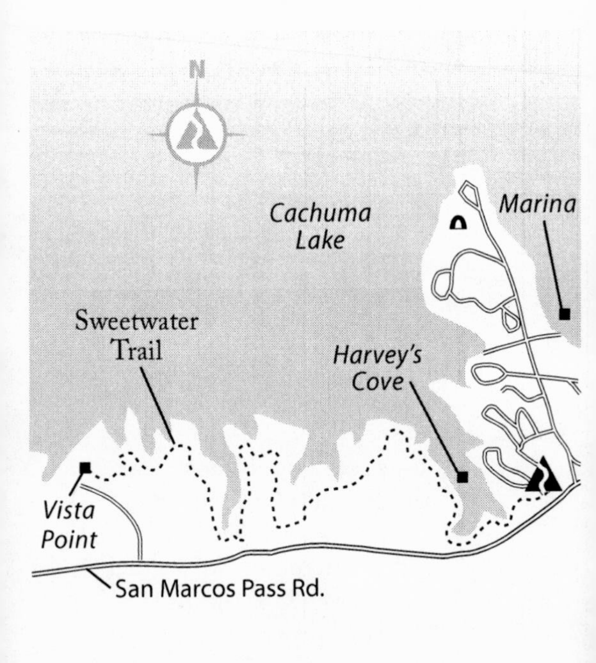
N
Cachuma Lake
Marina
Sweetwater Trail
Harvey's Cove
Vista Point
San Marcos Pass Rd.

SANTA YNEZ RIVER

Santa Ynez River Trail

From Red Rock Trailhead to Gibraltar Dam is 6 miles round trip with 400-foot elevation gain

Great swimming holes await hikers who venture to the attractive Santa Ynez Recreation Area. During dry years, the river's swimming holes are filled by releases from Gibraltar Reservoir, located up-river from the recreation area. Some pools maintain year-round depths of 6 to 18 feet.

Santa Ynez River Trail leads to several pleasant swimming holes and is an easy hike, suitable for the whole family. The most popular ol' swimmin' hole is Red Rock Pool, located only a short distance from the trailhead.

Don't look for solitude along the Santa Ynez River recreation areas. Red Rock and other swim spots are crowd magnets. On a warm weekend, get to the trailhead as early as you can.

DIRECTIONS: From Highway 101 in Santa Barbara, drive east on Highway 154 for about 10 miles. A short distance over the pass, just past a Vista Point, turn right on Paradise Road and drive 10.5 miles to the end of the road. Leave your car in the large dirt parking lot adjacent to the trail, which begins at a locked gate.

If you're the kind of hiker who loves loop trips, note the presence of a second trail leading from the parking lot to Gibraltar Dam. The "High Road," as its known by locals, makes a gentle traverse across the mountains above the river. Like the "low road," Santa Ynez River Trail, it's about three miles long. It's a good trail to keep in mind for times of high water.

THE HIKE: Wide, flat Santa Ynez River Trail crosses the river in 0.25. mile crosses the river. Soon after the first river crossing, you'll reach Red Rock, the most popular swimming hole.

The trail passes through oak woodland and zigzags from bank to bank along the river. Alongside the river is a canopy of cottonwood, sycamore and willow.

Wildlife viewing opportunities, particularly during the early morning hours, are quite good near the Santa Ynez River because the area includes several different habitats: oak woodland, coastal sage scrub, grassland and freshwater marsh. You might spot a deer, gray fox, striped skunk, lizard, cottontail rabbit or raccoon. Watch for pond turtles basking on the rocks, logs and banks of large pools.. In the woodland areas, birders might sight a quail, warbling vireo, northern oriole or a woodpecker. Cliff swallows and belted kingfishers swoop over the river.

Several more dry river crossings and a couple of wet ones, plus some travel beneath the boughs of handsome coast live oaks, will bring you to an oak shaded picnic area, located a few hundred yards down-river from the dam.

You may continue up the trail to Gibraltar Dam, named for the large rock here, which is said to resemble the great guardian rock of the Mediterranean. A second, shadeless picnic site is located at the southeast top edge of the dam. Observe the warning signs at the dam and stay out of restricted areas.

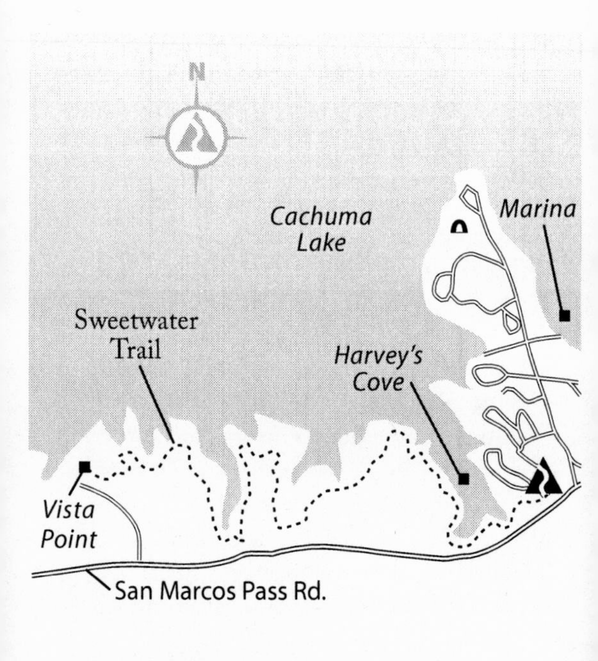
N
Cachuma
Lake
Marina
Sweetwater
Trail
Harvey's
Cove
Vista
Point
San Marcos Pass Rd.

Cachuma Lake

Sweetwater Trail

From Harvey Cove to Vista Point is 5 miles round trip

Cachuma Lake, besides storing an important part of Santa Barbara's water supply, is a popular weekend destination for Southland anglers, campers, bird watchers and hikers.

The Trailmaster recommends that after you hit the trail, you board a boat. Cachuma Lake's naturalist-led cruises explore the lake's waterfowl and wildlife. Join a tour in winter and you'll likely sight the migrating bald eagles that take up temporary residence at the lake.

While touring and hiking, you'll be delighted by the great multitude of birds—the flocks of geese taking flight or the clouds of canvasbacks traveling in long, V-shaped formations. You're almost certain to see the canvasback, a diving duck with a white back, rust-red head and long black bill. Likewise the bufflehead, one of the smallest diving ducks, a chubby white fellow with a black back that buzzes more like a fly than a bird.

The lake's longest-legged resident is the great blue heron. Its long neck, regal bearing, great size and its habit of standing motionless for long periods on one leg makes it an easy photo target.

Cachuma Lake's trail system is not extensive but does offer a unique perspective on the lake and its many species of waterfowl. Those bird watchers who hit the trail will glimpse numerous perching birds in the park's oak woodland: acorn woodpeckers, Western bluebirds, goldfinches, juncos and lots of sparrows.

The lake's Nature Center, headquartered in a 1930s ranch house, has displays about the ecology and history of the Santa Ynez Valley. Exhibits highlight birds, fish, local flora, and the native Chumash who once lived where the lake is today.

The park's best trail is the Sweetwater, which meanders lakeside through an oak woodland to a vista point for a commanding panorama of Cachuma. Oak Canyon Trail, a nature trail, extends 0.75 mile from the Nature Center to the Sweetwater Trail.

DIRECTIONS: From Highway 101 in Santa Barbara, exit on Highway 154 and drive 20 miles to the lake. Past the entry kiosk, turn left and follow the signs a half mile to Harvey Cove, where you'll find parking for a dozen cars and signed Sweetwater Trail.

THE HIKE: The first one hundred yards of trail is a paved wheelchair-access route that leads to an oak-shaded picnic area and the Harvey Cove dock. From here, a dirt path follows the far side of the cove for 0.25 mile before angling left into a handsome oak woodland.

A bit more than a mile's hike brings you to Sweetwater Cove, a tiny picnic area perched above the lake. The path joins a dirt road then, as it approaches Highway 154, resumes as a footpath that yo-yos up and down through oak forest before delivering you to Vista Point.

Enjoy the commanding view of Cachuma Lake, bordered on the south by the Santa Ynez Mountains, the north by the San Rafael range, then return the way you came.

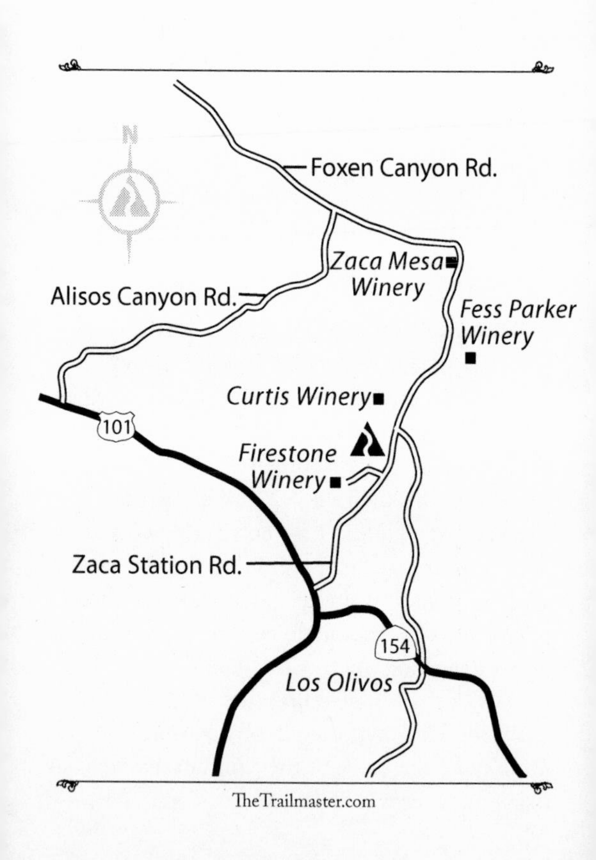
N
Foxen Canyon Rd.
Zaca Mesa
Winery
Alisos Canyon Rd.
Fess Parker
Winery
Curtis Winery
101
Firestone
Winery
Zaca Station Rd.
154
Los Olivos

FIRESTONE VINEYARD

Brooks' Trail

From Firestone Vineyard to Curtis Winery is 2.4 miles round trip

Perched atop a commanding mesa overlooking Zaca Canyon, the Santa Ynez Valley and the wilderness beyond, Firestone Vineyard is the oldest (established in 1972) estate winery in Santa Barbara County. The large (by valley standards) winery produces acclaimed Merlots, Chardonnays and Rieslings.

During the 1990s, winery founder Brooks Firestone represented the county in the State Assembly for a few terms, before returning to expand the family business. From the earliest days of wine touring in the Santa Ynez Valley, Firestone Vineyard has been a major player and a must-stop for wine-tasters.

Hikers were pleased when Firestone constructed "Brooks' Trail" around the vineyard. The pleasant pathway connects Firestone Vineyard with Curtis Winery. Plan your hike for a time when Firestone Vineyard's tasting room is open, usually 10 A.M. to 5 P.M. daily. For a little more wine country hiking, pay a visit to Zaca Mesa Winery, which occupies a scenic plateau overlooking Foxen Canyon. The winery offers tastings and two short trails. Windmill Trail (0.25 mile) climbs to a picnic area then up to a little overlook. Z Trail (0.25 mile) also climbs to an overlook, a popular promontory for exchanging wedding vows.

If you're fantasizing about hiking across the valley from winery to winery and stopping at each tasting room along the trail, you're going to be disappointed. Sauntering through vineyards in the valley is just not possible or even encouraged like it is in Provence and Tuscany.

Zaca Mesa and Firestone are among the few wineries where hikers can walk private reserves as well as taste them. We hikers are grateful for this small sampling of Santa Ynez Valley Wine

Country trails, but the valley is so beautiful and enticing, we're left thirsting for more.

DIRECTIONS: From Highway 101, some 45 miles north of Santa Barbara, exit on State Highway 154 and head east 2.5 miles to Foxen Canyon Road. Turn left and follow the winding road 4.4 miles to a junction with Zaca Station Road. Firestone Vineyard is located 0.7 mile south on Zaca Station Road. Curtis Winery is just west on the continuation of Foxen Canyon Road.

THE HIKE: The signed path begins by the picnic area, located just below the Firestone tasting room. Valley vistas are superb from the start of the trail. The trail descends to the vineyard, skirts rows and rows of grapes, and soon crosses the vineyard's paved entry road.

Sometimes brush-overgrown Brooks' Trail climbs a bit, then contours along oak-dotted slopes. Enjoy grand views of Foxen Canyon and the greater wine country. The sights and sounds of cars traveling Foxen Canyon and the rise and dip of active oil rigs amidst the rows of grape are also part of the valley scene. The path descends to Curtis Winery.

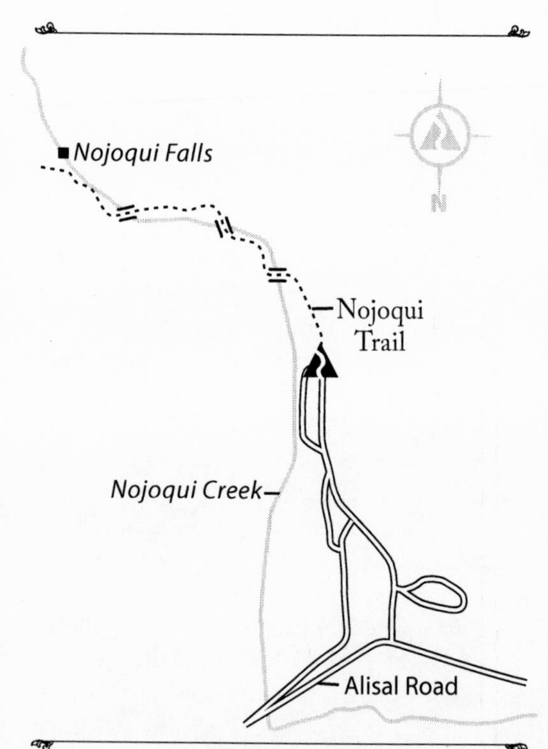
Nojoqui Falls
Nojoqui
Trail
N
Nojoqui Creek
Alisal Road

Nojoqui Falls

Nojoqui Falls Trail

To Falls is 0.5 mile round trip

Winter and spring are the seasons to sojourn to Nojoqui Falls, Santa Barbara County's highest and most dramatic waterfalls. Hidden in an isolated canyon near Solvang, Nojoqui Falls County Park is a great rest stop or picnic spot for drives along Highway 101.

DIRECTIONS: Follow Highway 101 a few miles north of Gaviota Pass, exit on Alisal Road and continue 1.5 miles to Nojoqui Falls County Park. (From Solvang, follow Alisal Road 6.5 miles south to the park.)

THE HIKE: A wide path leads through the shady canyon. After crossing three bridges over Nojoqui Creek, you reach the 80-foot falls, cascading over a mossy, fern-covered wall into a pretty little grotto.

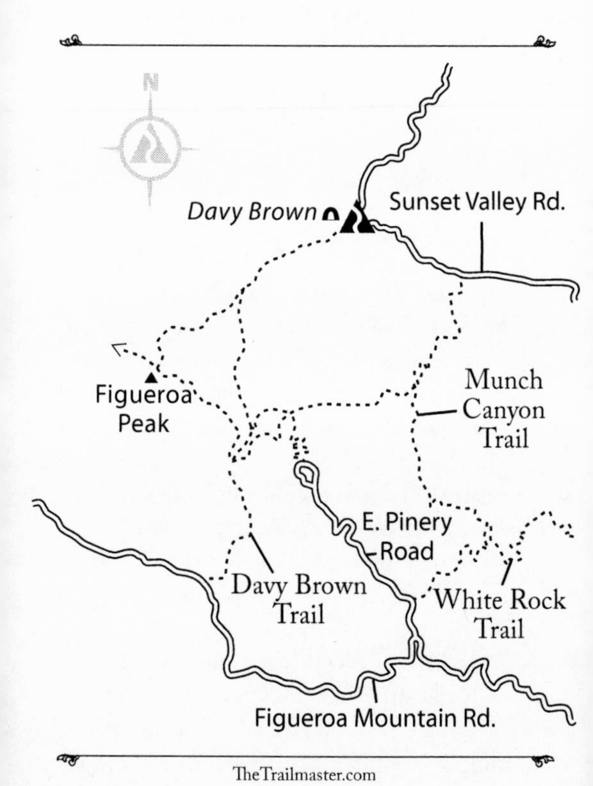
N
Davy Brown
Sunset Valley Rd.
Figueroa Peak
Munch Canyon Trail
E. Pinery Road
Davy Brown Trail
White Rock Trail
Figueroa Mountain Rd.

Fir Canyon and Figueroa Mountain

Davy Brown Trail

From Davy Brown Camp to Harry Roberts Cabin is 3.5 miles round trip with 900-foot elevation gain; to Figueroa Mt. Rd.is 6.25 miles round trip with 1,700-foot gain; to Figueroa Mt. Lookout is 7.5 miles round trip with 2,400-foot gain

Figueroa Mountain, located 25 air miles behind Santa Barbara in Los Padres National Forest, beckons the hiker with varieties of pines, oaks and abundant spring wildflowers.

Davy Brown Trail explores cool, moist Fir Canyon as well as the mountain's flora and colorful history. Link trails between Davy Brown Campground and Figueroa Mountain to make a variety of loop routes.

DIRECTIONS: Santa Barbara, follow Highway 154 past Lake Cachuma to Armour

Ranch Road. Turn right and drive 1.3 miles to Happy Canyon Road. Make a right and wind 14 miles to Cachuma Saddle Station. To reach the lower Davy Brown trailhead, bear right at the saddle onto Sunset Valley Road and drive 5 miles to Davy Brown Campground. To reach upper Davy Brown trailhead, bear left at Cachuma Saddle Station onto Figueroa Mountain Road and drive 5 miles to a turnout and signed Davy Brown Trail on the right. (Also gain access to both trailheads by exiting Highway 101 north of the Buellton turnoff on Highway 154, turning left on Figueroa Mountain Road and driving 15 miles to the upper trailhead.)

THE HIKE: From the northwest end of Davy Brown Camp, pass a gate and follow the road to the right, hiking down-creek past a number of swimming holes. About 0.75 mile out, you'll head west through forested Munch Canyon, cross Davy Brown Creek a couple of times, then begin angling southwest up Fir Canyon. (No firs grow in Fir Canyon but its cousin, big cone spruce, thrives.)

About 1.75 miles from the trailhead, you'll descend into an oak-shaded draw and arrive at the ruins of chrome miner Harry Roberts' cabin, built in the 1920s. Maple-shaded Davy Brown Trail crosses and re-crosses the creek. Keep a sharp lookout right for the unsigned side trail leading to Figueroa Mountain Lookout.

To follow Davy Brown Trail to its end, continue ascending along the creek. A half-mile from the top of the trail, step carefully around the Devil's Elbow, a splintered white Monterey shale outcropping at a point where the canyon makes a sharp turn. The trail climbs to the headwaters of Davy Brown Creek, then out onto a grassy slope dotted with pine and buttercups. Trail's end is Figueroa Mountain Road.

Figueroa Mountain Lookout-bound hikers will head right at the above-mentioned junction. The path climbs steeply onto a drier slope cloaked in chaparral, descends a short distance to a tiny meadow, then immediately climbs again.

The trail intersects a road to Figueroa Peak. Bear left and walk a half-mile to the lookout. Great vistas of peaks, coast, and islands.

N
Lost Valley Trail
NIRA
Lost Valley
Manzana Trail
Fish
Davy Brown
Manzana
Manzana Narrows
Sunset Valley Rd.

Manzana Creek

Manzana Creek Trail

From NIRA to Lost Valley Camp is 2 miles round trip with 100-foot elevation gain; to Fish Creek Camp is 6 miles round trip with 400-foot gain; to Manzana Camp is 6.5 miles round trip with 1,100-foot gain; to Manzana Narrows is 14 miles round trip with 1,200-foot gain

San Rafael Wilderness was the first Wilderness Area set aside under the federal Wilderness Act of 1964. "San Rafael is rocky, rugged, wooded and lonely," President Lyndon B. Johnson remarked when he signed the bill. "I believe it will enrich the spirit of America."

Manzana Creek Trail begins at NIRA, an auto camp, popular day-use area and major entry point for the wilderness. The trail links four creekside camps. Rewarding the hiker after many stream crossings is Manzana Narrows, with fine pools for fishing and cooling off. (Manzana Creek can be impassable in times of high water.)

DIRECTIONS: From U.S.101 in Santa Barbara, exit on California 154 and follow the latter highway over San Marcos Pass. Beyond Lake Cachuma, turn right on Armour Ranch Road and proceed 2.5 miles to Happy Canyon Road. Make another right and continue 17 miles (Happy Canyon Road becomes Sunset Valley Road after passing an intersection at Figueroa Mountain Road) to NIRA Camp. Parking space for hikers is provided at the south end of the campground. The trail departs from a large sign marking the San Rafael Wilderness Area.

THE HIKE: Leaving NIRA Camp, the trail soon crosses Manzana Creek and begins a gentle ascent along the north bank of the creek. The route switchbacks up a low ridge, cloaked with gray pine and soon arrives at Lost Valley Camp, a small site tucked among oak and pine at the mouth of Lost Valley Canyon. (Lost Valley Trail departs from camp and climbs up to magnificent Hurricane Deck, heart of the wilderness.)

Manzana Creek Trail meanders along the north bank of the creek for the next 2 miles.

Look to your right across the creek and you'll spot Fish Creek Camp on the far side of the Manzana flood plain, where Fish Creek meets Manzana Creek. Fishermen like this camp because the creeks here host a large trout population.

Past Fish Creek, Manzana Creek Trail at first stays on the north wall of the canyon, passing through chaparral and dipping in and out of washes. Manzana Canyon narrows and the trail angles down toward the creek, which is lined by tall thin alders. The trail crosses the Manzana, and 0.5 mile later, crosses again. The canyon narrows even more and, after a few more creek crossings, the path brings you to Manzana Camp. The camp offers a dependable water supply, fishing and swimming pools. Manzanita, which gave its name to half the geographical features around here, abounds.

Beyond this camp, the trail switchbacks up onto the east wall of the canyon, then soon descends to Manzana Narrows Camp. Wedged in the narrow canyon, the oak- and willow-shaded camp offers pools for fishing and cooling off.

JOHN MCKINNEY, HIKING EXPERT

John McKinney is the author of 25 books about hiking, parklands and nature, including ***The Hiker's Way*** and ***A Walk Along Land's End: Dispatches from the Edge of California on a 1,600-mile hike from Mexico to Oregon.***

HIKE Smart and ***HIKE for Health & Fitness*** are among the debut titles in The Trailmaster's Minibuk series, designed to give hikers the information they need in an engaging and easily accessible way.

For 18 years, he wrote a weekly hiking column for the ***Los Angeles Times***, and has hiked and enthusiastically described more than ten thousand miles of trail across America and around the world. John, a.k.a.The Trailmaster, has written more than a thousand articles about hiking plus numerous trail guidebooks, including ***Southern California: A Day Hiker's Guide*** and ***Day Hiker's Guide to California's State Parks.***

A passionate advocate for hiking and our need to reconnect with nature, John McKinney shares his expertise on radio, TV, online, and as a public speaker.

HIKE ON.

www.TheTrailmaster.com